One-Digit Addition and Subtraction with Cuisenaire Rods

BY PATRICIA S. DAVIDSON

Cuisenaire Company of America, Inc.
10 Bank Street. P.O. Box 5026
White Plains, NY 10602-5026

This workbook is part of the
CUISENAIRE LEARNING EXPERIENCE SERIES

It is intended to be used in conjunction with the
Teacher Resource Guide for One-Digit Addition
and Subtraction with Cuisenaire Rods

Copyright© 1978 by
Cuisenaire Company of America, Inc.
10 Bank Street, PO Box 5026, White Plains, NY 10602-5026

ISBN 0-914040-21-9

4 5 6 7 8 9-BK-00

Workbook Contents

★ The star indicates that this worksheet has been left open-ended so that the teacher or children may pose additional problems as needed.

Name _____

"Put rods on each picture so that they match."

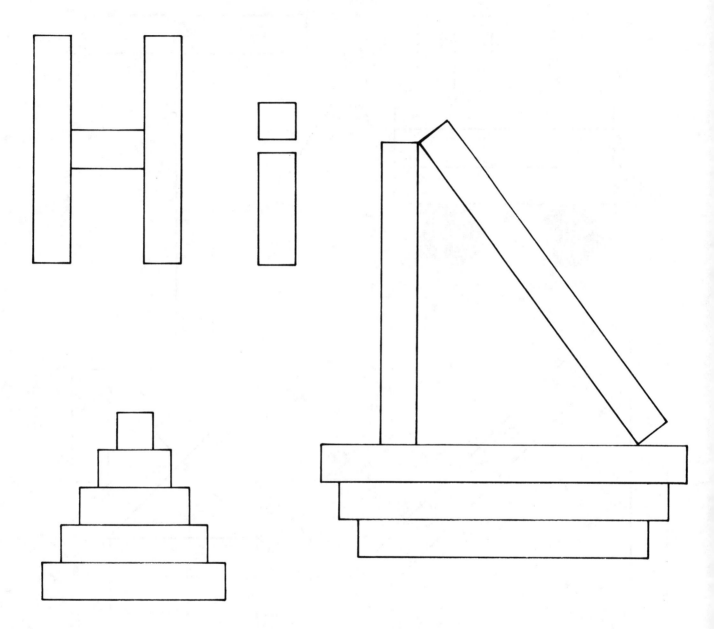

"Remove each rod.

Color the pictures with the correct rod colors."

Commentary in Teacher Resource Guide, p.31
One-Digit Addition and Subtraction with Cuisenaire Rods
Cuisenaire Company of America, Inc. Copyright © 1978

Name_____

"Put the rods on their pictures."

"Remove each rod.

Color the pictures with the correct rod colors."

Commentary in Teacher Resource Guide, p. 31
One-Digit Addition and Subtraction with Cuisenaire Rods
Cuisenaire Company of America, Inc. Copyright © 1978

Name_____

"Write the correct code for each rod.

Color the pictures with the correct rod colors."

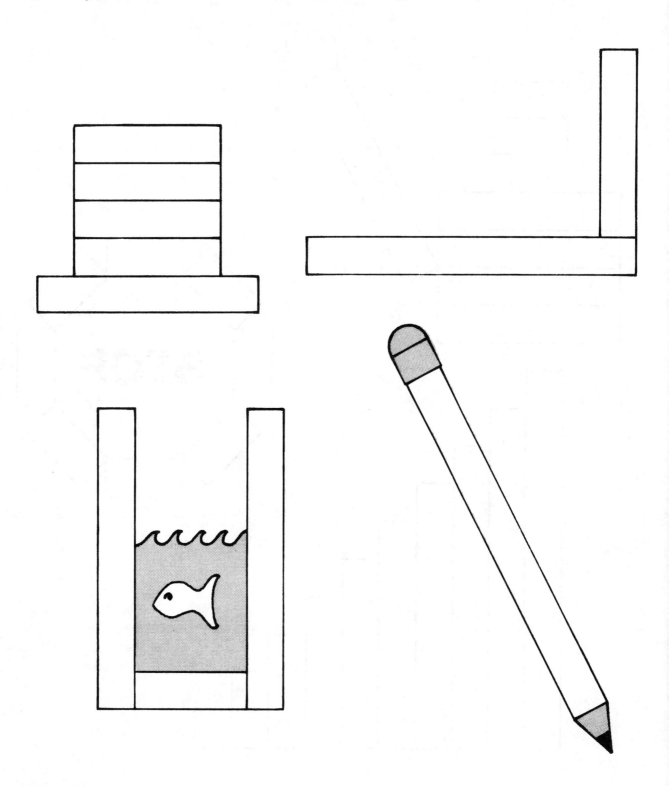

Commentary in Teacher Resource Guide, p.45
One-Digit Addition and Subtraction with Cuisenaire Rods
Cuisenaire Company of America, Inc. Copyright © 1978

Name_____

"Write the correct code for each rod.
Color the pictures with the correct rod colors."

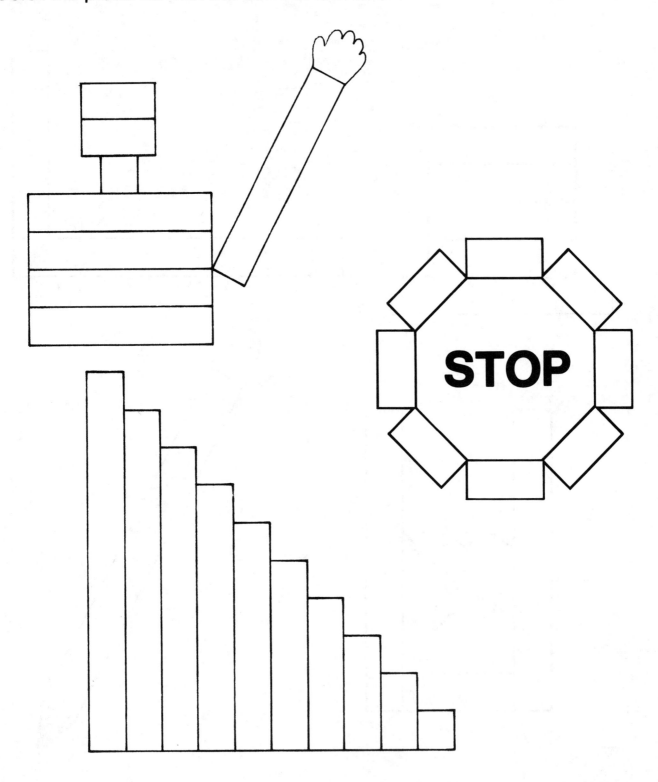

Practicing Rod Codes

Commentary in Teacher Resource Guide, p. 45
One-Digit Addition and Subtraction with Cuisenaire Rods
Cuisenaire Company of America, Inc. Copyright © 1978

Name _____

"Put the rod for each code on the strip.
Color its length."

Example:

D . . . . .

① P . . . . .

② K . . . . .

③ R . . . . .

④ Y . . . . .

⑤ G . . . . .

⑥ Ơ . . . . .

⑦ N . . . . .

Name _____

"Color the length of the rod for each code.
Do not use rods."

Example:

K . . . . . [▨▨▨▨▨░░░░░░░░░░]

① P . . . . . [ ][ ][ ][ ][ ][ ][ ][ ][ ][ ][ ][ ][ ][ ][ ]

② W . . . . . [ ][ ][ ][ ][ ][ ][ ][ ][ ][ ][ ][ ][ ][ ][ ]

③ D . . . . . [ ][ ][ ][ ][ ][ ][ ][ ][ ][ ][ ][ ][ ][ ][ ]

④ R . . . . . [ ][ ][ ][ ][ ][ ][ ][ ][ ][ ][ ][ ][ ][ ][ ]

⑤ O . . . . . [ ][ ][ ][ ][ ][ ][ ][ ][ ][ ][ ][ ][ ][ ][ ]

⑥ N . . . . . [ ][ ][ ][ ][ ][ ][ ][ ][ ][ ][ ][ ][ ][ ][ ]

⑦ E . . . . . [ ][ ][ ][ ][ ][ ][ ][ ][ ][ ][ ][ ][ ][ ][ ]

"Check your answers with the rods."

Name _____

"Cover each rod picture with white rods.
  Circle the number of white rods used."
Color the rod pictures with the correct colors."

Example:

3   (4)   5   6

① _____   5 6 7 8

② _____   8 9 10 11

③ __   2 3 4 5

④ ____   2 3 4 5

⑤ _____   7 8 9 10

⑥ __   1 2 3 4

⑦ _____   5 6 7 8

Name _____

"Cover each rod picture with white rods.

Draw a line from each rod picture to the number of white rods that cover it.

Color the rod pictures with the correct colors."

Example:

1

①   2

②   3

③   4

④   5

⑤   6

⑥   7

⑦   8

⑧   9

⑨   10

Matching Rods and Numerals

Commentary in Teacher Resource Guide, p.51
One-Digit Addition and Subtraction with Cuisenaire Rods
Cuisenaire Company of America, Inc. Copyright © 1978

Worksheet **8**

Name _____

"Find the rod that matches each train of white rods.
Color the length with the correct rod color."

Example:

6W

① 9W

② 2W

③ 5W

④ 10W

⑤ 3W

⑥ 8W

⑦ 4W

⑧ 7W

"Check your answers with rods."

Name _____

"Find one rod that matches each train of white rods.
Color the length with the correct rod color."

Example:

4W

① 8W

② 3W

③ 5W

④ 7W

⑤ 6W

⑥ 10W

⑦ 2W

⑧ 9W

"Check your answers with rods."

Coloring Rod Lengths
Commentary in Teacher Resource Guide, p.53
One-Digit Addition and Subtraction with Cuisenaire Rods
Cuisenaire Company of America, Inc. Copyright © 1978

Worksheet 10

Name _____

"Color the correct length for each rod code.
Do not use rods."

Example:

R . . . . . [▨][ ][ ][ ][ ][ ][ ][ ][ ][ ][ ][ ][ ]

① P . . . . . [ ][ ][ ][ ][ ][ ][ ][ ][ ][ ][ ][ ][ ][ ]

② ♂ . . . . . [ ][ ][ ][ ][ ][ ][ ][ ][ ][ ][ ][ ][ ][ ]

③ K . . . . . [ ][ ][ ][ ][ ][ ][ ][ ][ ][ ][ ][ ][ ][ ]

④ W . . . . . [ ][ ][ ][ ][ ][ ][ ][ ][ ][ ][ ][ ][ ][ ]

⑤ E . . . . . [ ][ ][ ][ ][ ][ ][ ][ ][ ][ ][ ][ ][ ][ ]

⑥ Y . . . . . [ ][ ][ ][ ][ ][ ][ ][ ][ ][ ][ ][ ][ ][ ]

⑦ G . . . . . [ ][ ][ ][ ][ ][ ][ ][ ][ ][ ][ ][ ][ ][ ]

"Check your answers with rods."

Commentary in Teacher Resource Guide, p.55
One-Digit Addition and Subtraction with Cuisenaire Rods
Cuisenaire Company of America, Inc. Copyright © 1978

This blank page indicates a break in the sequence of worksheets. Refer to the Teacher Resource Guide for the Learning Experiences which follow.

Name _____

"Write the code for the rod that matches each train
of white rods."

┌─ Example: ───┐
│   │
│ | 2W | 9W | 6W | │
│ |----|----|----| │
│ | R | E | D | │
│   │
└───┘

① | 3W | 10 W | 10 W | 6 W | ② | 6 W | 10 W | 3 W |
  | | | | | | | | |

③ | 3 W | 10W | ④ | 6 W | 10 W | 1 W | 8 W |
  | | | | | | | |

Matching Numerals and Codes
Commentary in Teacher Resource Guide, p.57
One-Digit Addition and Subtraction with Cuisenaire Rods
Cuisenaire Company of America, Inc. Copyright © 1978

Name_____

"Write the code for the rod that matches each train
of white rods."

①
5W	10W	5W	10W

②
4W	9W	9W	7W

③
2W	10W	4W	9W

④
3W	2W	10W	1W

the ⑤
9W	8W	6W

Commentary in Teacher Resource Guide, p.57
One-Digit Addition and Subtraction with Cuisenaire Rods
Cuisenaire Company of America, Inc. Copyright ® 1978

Name _____

"Find one rod that matches each train of red rods.
Color the length with the correct rod color."

Example:

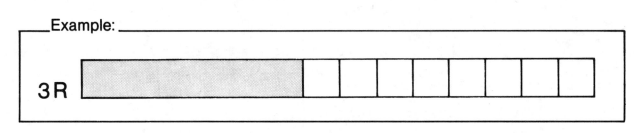

3R

① 1R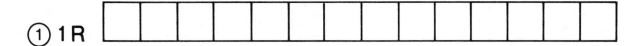

② 4R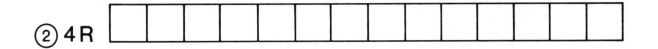

③ 2R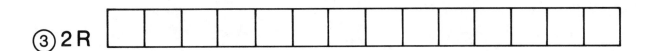

④ 5R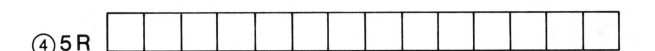

⑤ 3R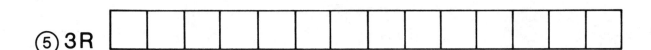

This blank page indicates a break in the sequence
of worksheets. Refer to the Teacher Resource
Guide for the Learning Experiences which follow.

Name _____

"Find a rod that is less than the rod shown.
Color the length of the rod that you have found."

Example:

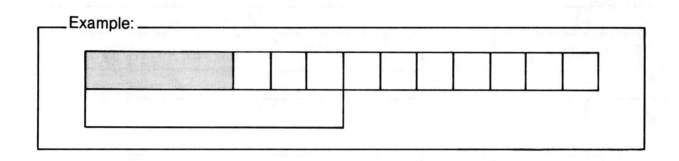

①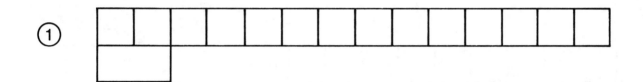

②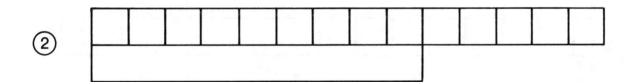

③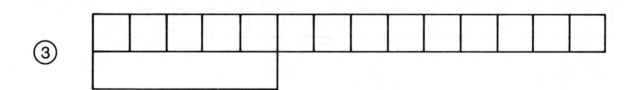

④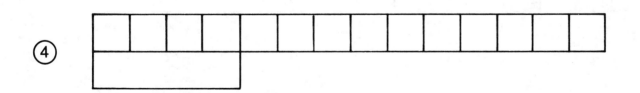

Commentary in Teacher Resource Guide, p.67
One-Digit Addition and Subtraction with Cuisenaire Rods
Cuisenaire Company of America, Inc. Copyright © 1978

Name _____

"Find a rod that is less than the rod shown.
Color the length of the rod that you have found."

Example:

①

②

③

④

⑤

Practicing Less Than
Commentary in Teacher Resource Guide, p.67
One-Digit Addition and Subtraction with Cuisenaire Rods
Cuisenaire Company of America, Inc. Copyright © 1978

Name _____

"Find the rod that matches this rod picture.
Circle and color all the pictures of rods
less than this rod."

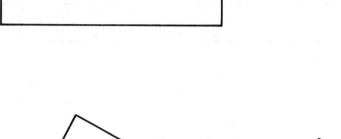

Commentary in Teacher Resource Guide, p.67
One-Digit Addition and Subtraction with Cuisenaire Rods
Cuisenaire Company of America, Inc. Copyright © 1978

Name _____

"Choose a rod.
Color its length on the strip.
Circle all pictures of rods that are less than this rod."

Name _____

"Find a rod that is greater than the rod shown.
 Color the length of the rod that you have found."

Example:

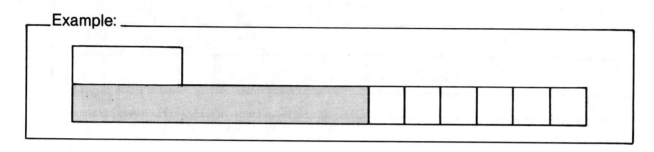

①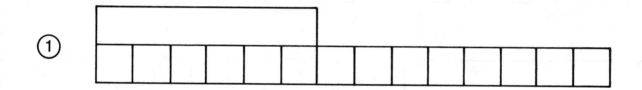

②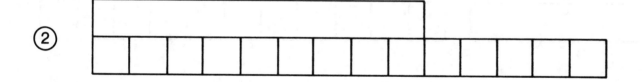

③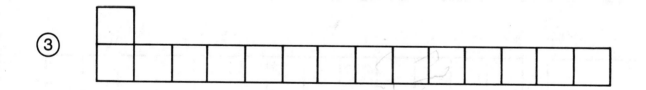

④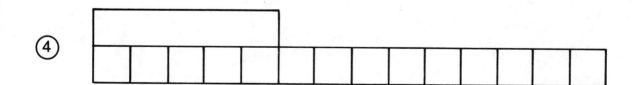

Name _____

"Find a rod that is greater than the rod shown.
Color the length of the rod that you have found."

Example:

①

②

③

④

⑤

Practicing Greater Than
Commentary in Teacher Resource Guide, p.71
One-Digit Addition and Subtraction with Cuisenaire Rods
Cuisenaire Company of America, Inc. Copyright © 1978

Name _____

"Find the rod that matches this rod picture.
Circle and color all the pictures of rods greater
than this rod."

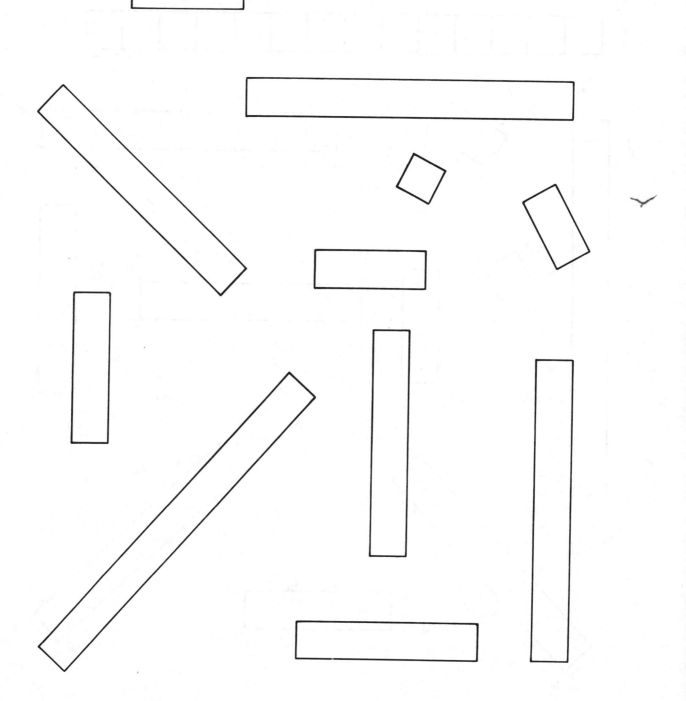

Commentary in Teacher Resource Guide, p. 71
One-Digit Addition and Subtraction with Cuisenaire Rods
Cuisenaire Company of America, Inc. Copyright © 1978

Name _____

"Choose a rod.

Color its length on the strip.

Circle all the pictures of rods that are greater than this rod."

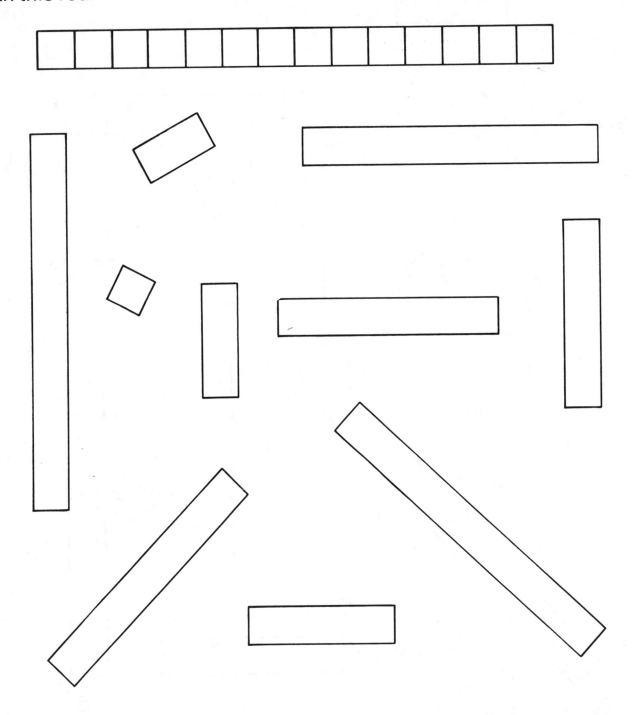

Practicing Greater Than
Commentary in Teacher Resource Guide, p.71
One-Digit Addition and Subtraction with Cuisenaire Rods
Cuisenaire Company of America, Inc. Copyright © 1978

Name _____

"Write the correct sign, < (less than) or > (greater than)."

Example:

	<	

①

②

③

④

⑤

Practicing Inequality Signs
Commentary in Teacher Resource Guide, p.77
One-Digit Addition and Subtraction with Cuisenaire Rods
Cuisenaire Company of America, Inc. Copyright © 1978

Name _____

"Find a rod to complete each inequality.
Color the length of the rod that you have found."

Example:

>

① <

② >

③ <

④ >

⑤ >

Practicing Inequality Signs
Commentary in Teacher Resource Guide, p.77
One-Digit Addition and Subtraction with Cuisenaire Rods
Cuisenaire Company of America, Inc. Copyright © 1978

Name _____

"Write the correct sign, < (less than) or > (greater than)."

┌─ Example: ──────────────────────────────────┐
│   │
│   3 _<_ 7   │
│   │
└──┘

    ①   5 _____ 9

    ②   7 _____ 4

    ③   6 _____ 7

    ④   10 _____ 8

    ⑤   2 _____ 1

"Check your answers with rods."

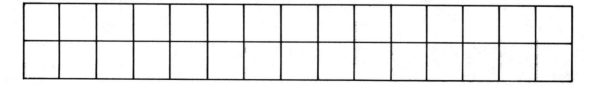

Practicing Inequality Signs
Commentary in Teacher Resource Guide, p.77
One-Digit Addition and Subtraction with Cuisenaire Rods
Cuisenaire Company of America, Inc. Copyright © 1978

Worksheet **25**

This blank page indicates a break in the sequence of worksheets. Refer to the Teacher Resource Guide for the Learning Experiences which follow.

"Find the rod that matches each rod picture.
Find all the two-car trains that match this rod.
Color the picture of the trains."

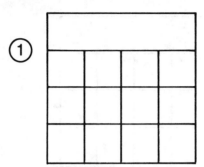

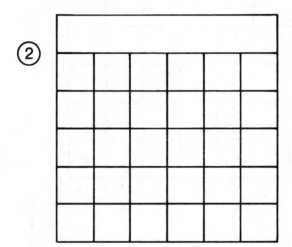

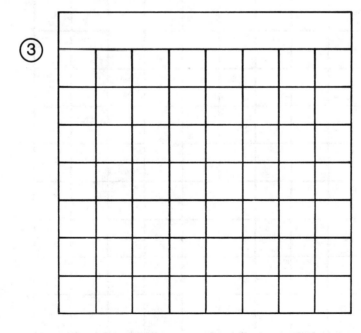

Finding All Two-Car Trains

Commentary in Teacher Resource Guide, p.83
One-Digit Addition and Subtraction with Cuisenaire Rods
Cuisenaire Company of America, Inc. Copyright © 1978

Worksheet **26**

Name _____

"Find the rod that matches each rod picture.
Find all the two-car trains that match this rod.
Color the pictures of the trains."

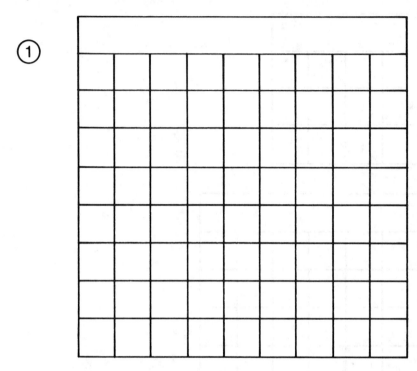

Commentary in Teacher Resource Guide, p.83
One-Digit Addition and Subtraction with Cuisenaire Rods
Cuisenaire Company of America, Inc. Copyright © 1978

Name _____

"Use codes to write the plus story for each train picture."

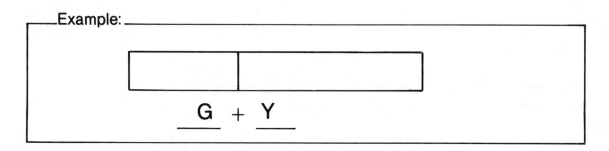

Example:

_G_ + _Y_

①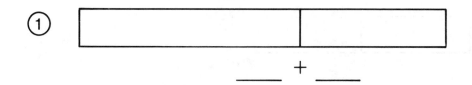

_____ + _____

②

_____ + _____

③

_____ + _____

④

_____ + _____ + _____

Commentary in Teacher Resource Guide, p.87
One-Digit Addition and Subtraction with Cuisenaire Rods
Cuisenaire Company of America, Inc. Copyright © 1978

Name _____

"Use codes to write the plus story for each train picture."

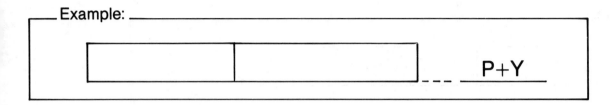
Example: P+Y

①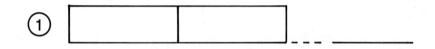

②

③

④

⑤

Practicing the Plus Sign
Commentary in Teacher Resource Guide, p.87
One-Digit Addition and Subtraction with Cuisenaire Rods
Cuisenaire Company of America, Inc. Copyright © 1978

Name _____

"Color the train picture for each plus story."

Example:

O+R

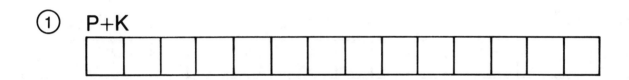

① P+K

② G+D

③ E+Y

④ R+W+R+W

Commentary in Teacher Resource Guide, p.87
One-Digit Addition and Subtraction with Cuisenaire Rods
Cuisenaire Company of America, Inc. Copyright © 1978

Name _____

"Color the train picture for each plus story."

K+E

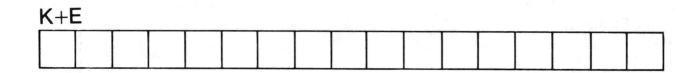

① O+P

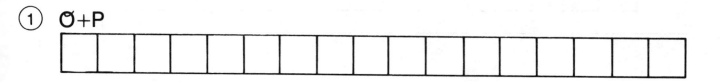

② N+D

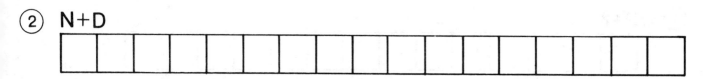

③ D+O

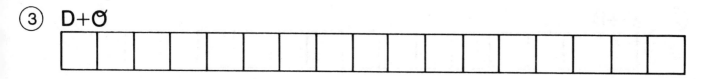

④ R+R+R+R

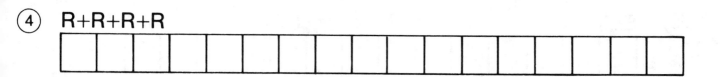

⑤ N+Y

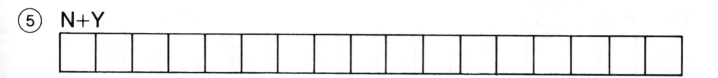

Name _____

"Find the rod that matches each train.
  Color the rod picture.
  Write the plus story."

Example:

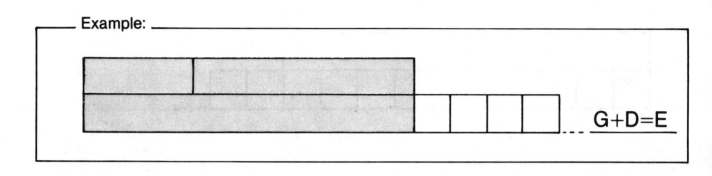

G+D=E

①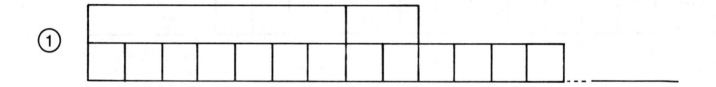

②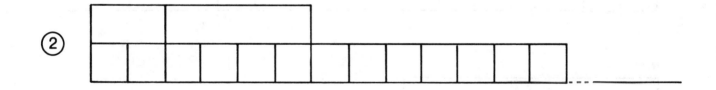

③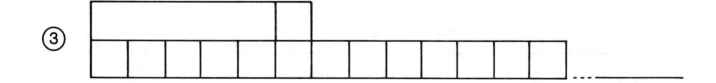

Commentary in Teacher Resource Guide, p.97
One-Digit Addition and Subtraction with Cuisenaire Rods
Cuisenaire Company of America, Inc. Copyright © 1978

Name _____

"Find the rod that matches each train.
Color the rod picture.
Write the plus story."

①

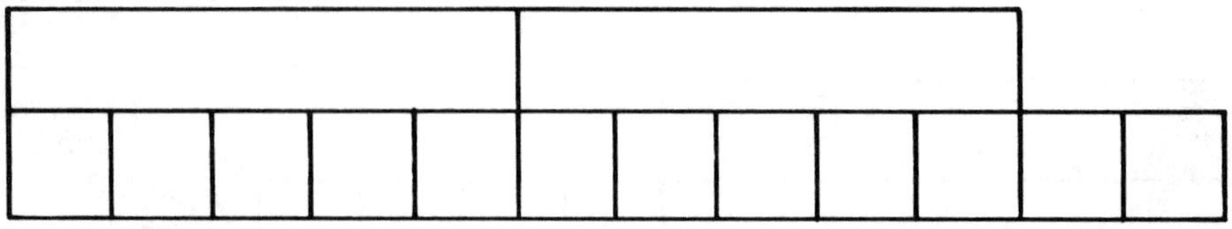

②

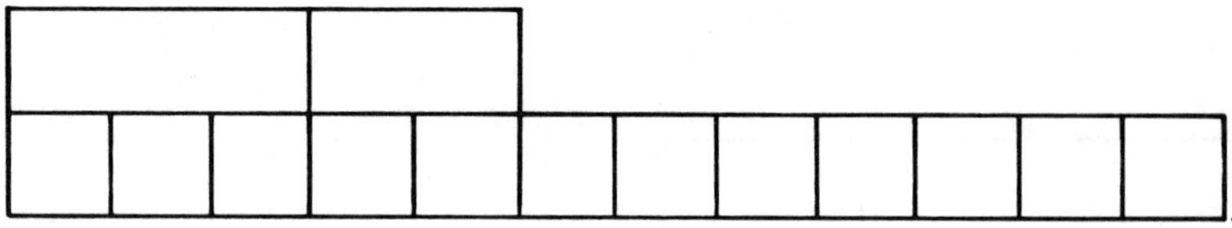

③

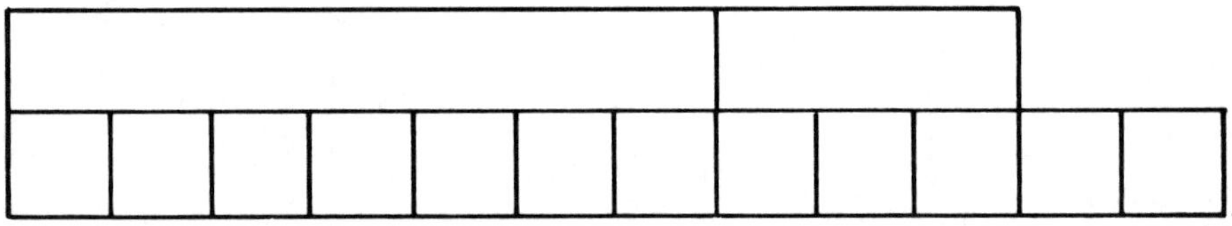

④

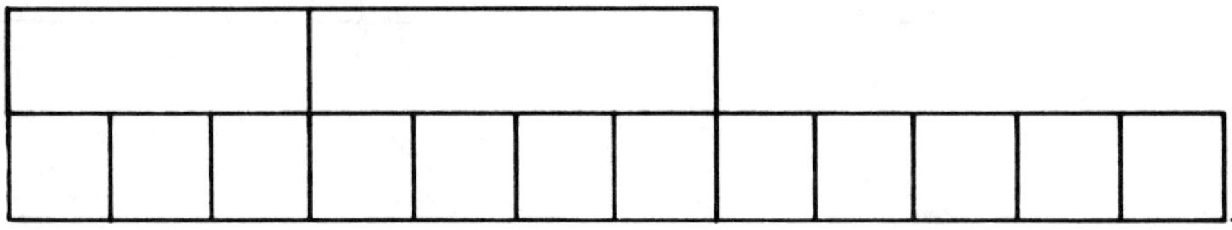

⑤

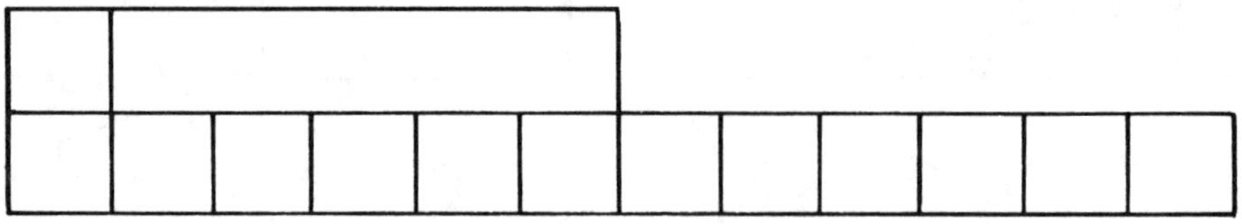

Name _____

"Color the train picture for each plus story.
  Find and color the length that matches each train.
  Use codes to write the complete plus story."

Example:

W+K

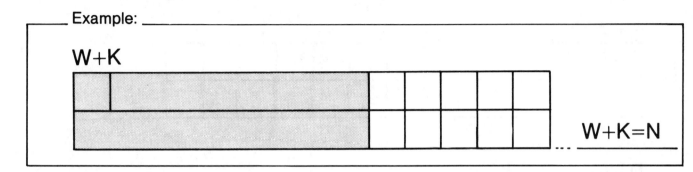

W+K=N

N+R

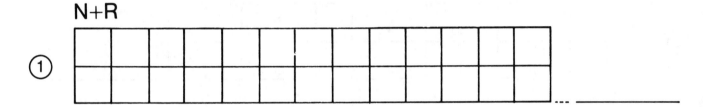

① _____

G+Y

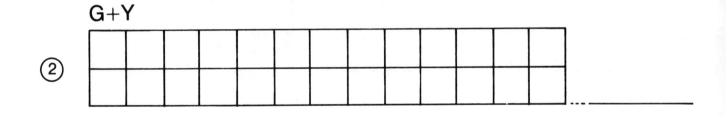

② _____

P+P

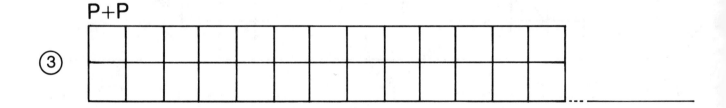

③ _____

R+W

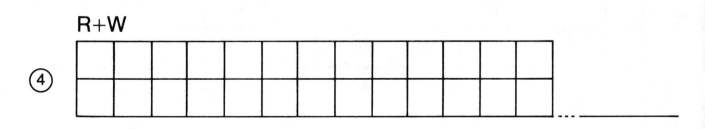

④ _____

Completing Plus Stories

Worksheet **34**

Commentary in Teacher Resource Guide, p.99
One-Digit Addition and Subtraction with Cuisenaire Rods
Cuisenaire Company of America, Inc. Copyright © 1978

Name _____

"Color the train picture for each plus story.
 Find and color the length that matches each train.
 Use codes to write the complete plus story."

Y+G

 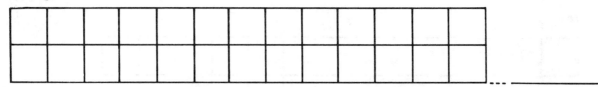

D+W

 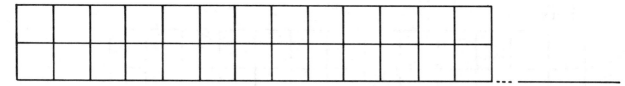

R+N

 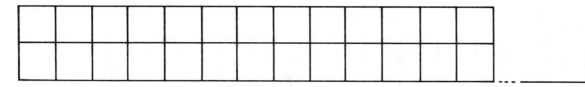

W+E

G+G+G

Completing Plus Stories
Commentary in Teacher Resource Guide, p.99
One-Digit Addition and Subtraction with Cuisenaire Rods
Cuisenaire Company of America, Inc. Copyright © 1978

Name _____

"Find all the trains that match the rod picture.
 Color the picture of each train.
 Write plus stories for your trains."

Example:

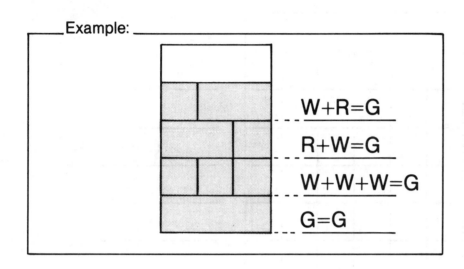

W+R=G

R+W=G

W+W+W=G

G=G

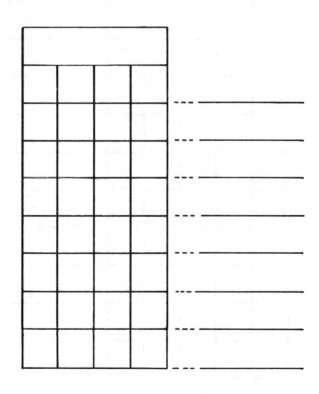

--- _____

--- _____

--- _____

--- _____

--- _____

--- _____

--- _____

--- _____

Finding Plus Story Patterns
Commentary in Teacher Resource Guide, p.101
One-Digit Addition and Subtraction with Cuisenaire Rods
Cuisenaire Company of America, Inc. Copyright © 1978

Name _____

"Find lots of different trains that match the orange rod.
   Color the picture of each train.
   Write plus stories for your trains."

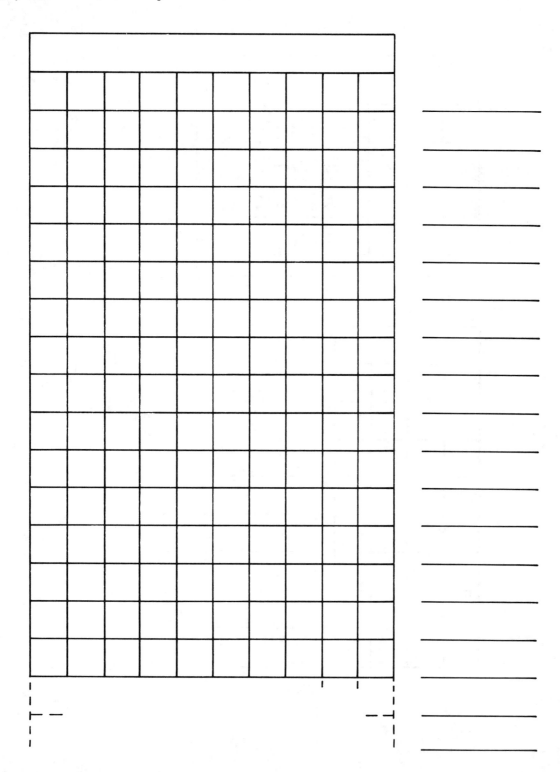

Name _____

"Find the rod that matches both trains.
 Color its length.
 Write a plus story for each train."

Example:

R+D=N _____

D+R=N _____

① _____

_____

② _____

_____

③ _____

_____

Commentary in Teacher Resource Guide, p.103
One-Digit Addition and Subtraction with Cuisenaire Rods
Cuisenaire Company of America, Inc. Copyright © 1978

This blank page indicates a break in the sequence of worksheets. Refer to the Teacher Resource Guide for the Learning Experiences which follow.

Name _____

"Find another plus story using the same three rods.
Use codes to write the new plus story."

Example:

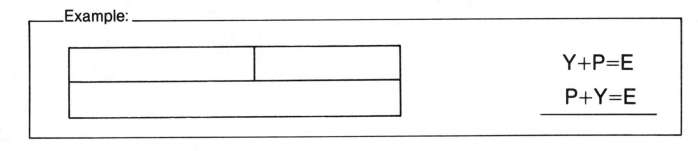

Y+P=E
P+Y=E
_____

①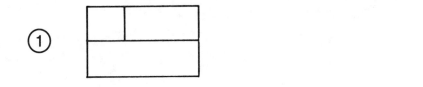

W+R=G

_____

②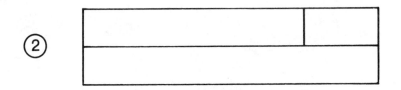

D+R=N

_____

③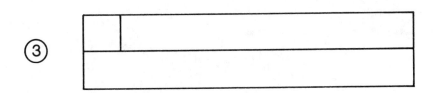

W+N=E

_____

④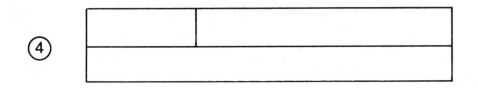

G+K=O̷

_____

Using the Same Three Rods
Commentary in Teacher Resource Guide, p.105
One-Digit Addition and Subtraction with Cuisenaire Rods

This blank page indicates a break in the sequence
of worksheets. Refer to the Teacher Resource
Guide for the Learning Experiences which follow.

Name _____

"Find the rod that matches each train.
Color its length.
Write an addition story."

Example:

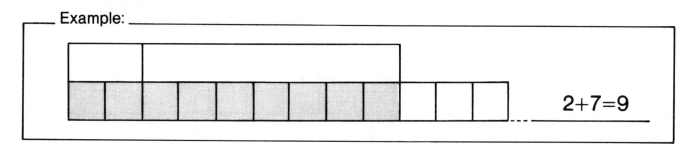

2+7=9

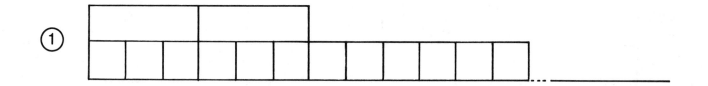

① _____

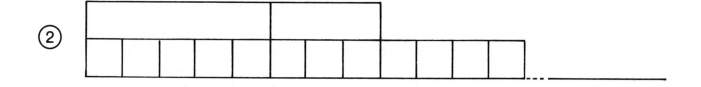

② _____

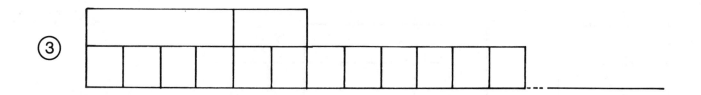

③ _____

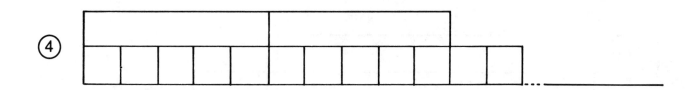

④ _____

Commentary in Teacher Resource Guide, p.109
One-Digit Addition and Subtraction with Cuisenaire Rods
Cuisenaire Company of America, Inc. Copyright © 1978

Name _____

"Find the single rod that matches each train.

Color its length.

Write an addition story."

①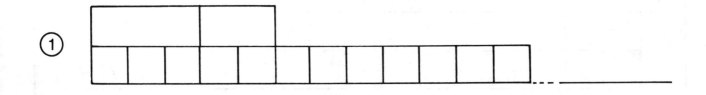

②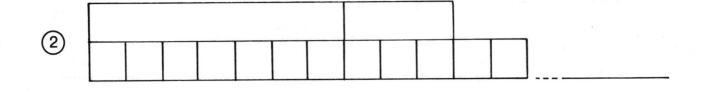

③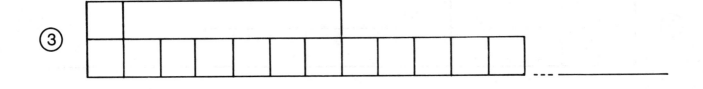

④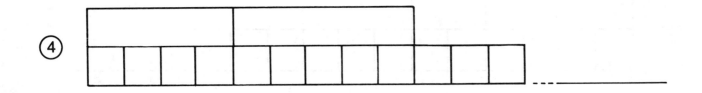

⑤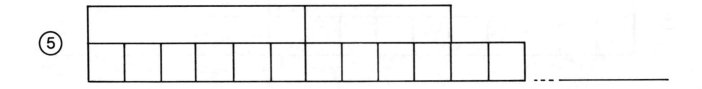

Writing Addition Stories
Commentary in Teacher Resource Guide, p.109
One-Digit Addition and Subtraction with Cuisenaire Rods
Cuisenaire Company of America, Inc. Copyright © 1978

Name _____

"Color each train.

Find and color the single length that matches the train.

Write an addition story."

┌─── Example: ──┐
│   │
│ P+G   │
│   │
│ 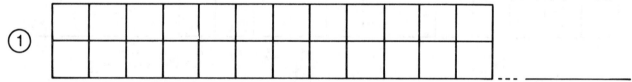   4+3=7   │
│   │
└───┘

W+Y

① _____

D+R

② _____

G+G

③ _____

Name _____

"Color each train.
Find and color the single length that matches the train.
Write an addition story."

G+R

① _____

Y+P

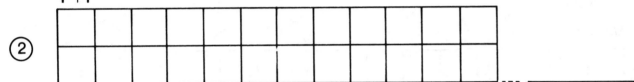

② _____

R+W

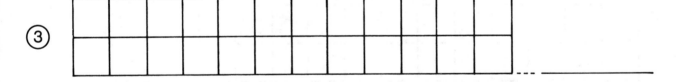

③ _____

P+D

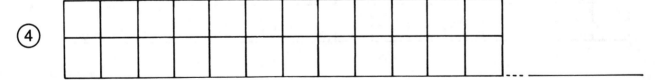

④ _____

Name _____

"Write the code for a train with two cars.
Color the train.
Find and color the length that matches the train.
Write an addition story."

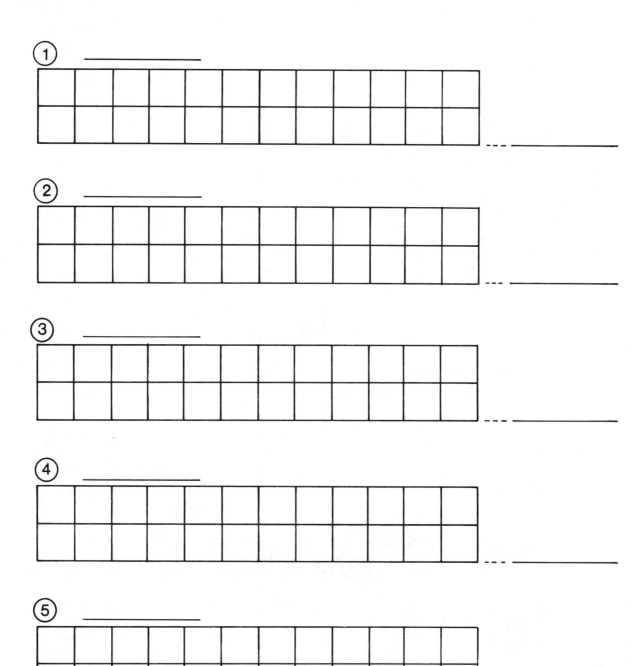

This blank page indicates a break in the sequence of worksheets. Refer to the Teacher Resource Guide for the Learning Experiences which follow.

Name _____

"Color a picture of the train to match each number story.
Color the single length that matches each train.
Complete the addition story."

Example:

2+3

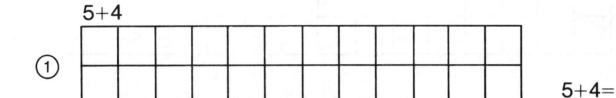

2+3=5

5+4

① 5+4=

1+7

② 1+7=

3+6

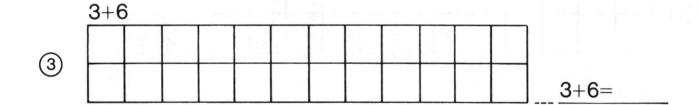

③ 3+6=

8+2

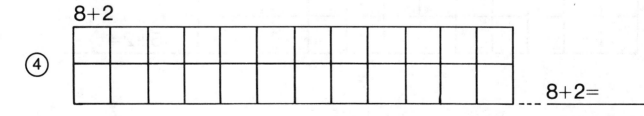

④ 8+2=

Finding Sums

Worksheet 45

Commentary in Teacher Resource Guide, p.113
One-Digit Addition and Subtraction with Cuisenaire Rods
Cuisenaire Company of America, Inc. Copyright © 1978

Name _____

"Color a picture of a train to match each number story.
  Color the single length that matches each train.
  Complete the addition story."

3+4

 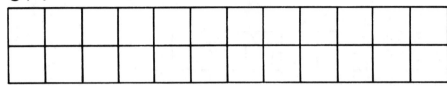

3+4= _____

5+5

 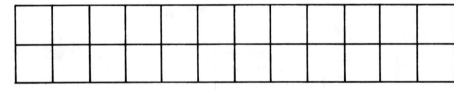

5+5= _____

4+1

 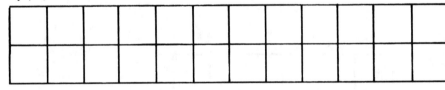

4+1= _____

2+6

 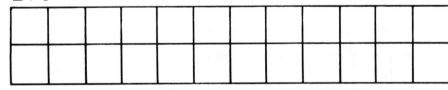

2+6= _____

5+2

 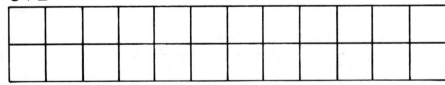

5+2= _____

Name _____

"Write a number story for addition.
Color a picture of the train to match the story.
Color the single length that matches each train.
Write the completed addition story."

① _____

② _____

③ _____

④ _____

⑤ _____

Finding Sums
Commentary in Teacher Resource Guide, p.113
One-Digit Addition and Subtraction with Cuisenaire Rods
Cuisenaire Company of America, Inc. Copyright © 1978

★Worksheet **47**

This blank page indicates a break in the sequence
of worksheets. Refer to the Teacher Resource
Guide for the Learning Experiences which follow.

Name _____

"Use rods on number lines to help find sums.
Complete the addition stories."

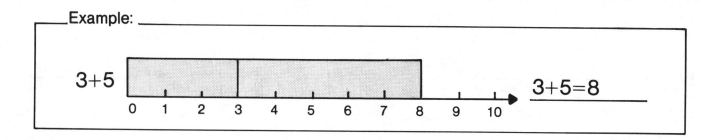

Example:

3+5   3+5=8

① 2+4   2+4=

② 8+1   8+1=

③ 7+3   7+3=

④ 4+6   4+6=

⑤ 1+5   1+5=

⑥ 4+4   4+4=

Name _____

"Write some number stories for addition.

Use rods on number lines to help find their sums.

Write completed addition stories."

① _____ 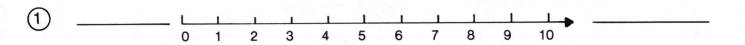 _____

② _____ 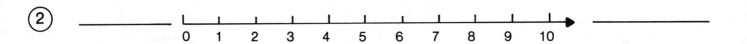 _____

③ _____ 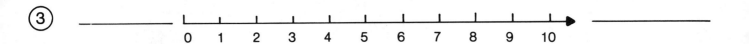 _____

④ _____ 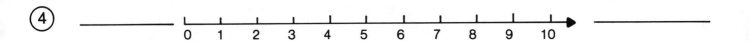 _____

⑤ _____ 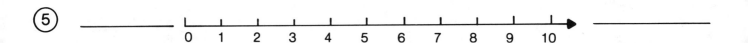 _____

⑥ _____ 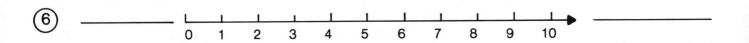 _____

⑦ _____ 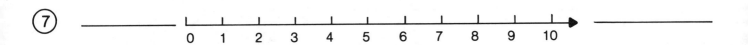 _____

Using Number Lines to Add
Commentary in Teacher Resource Guide, p.115
One-Digit Addition and Subtraction with Cuisenaire Rods
Cuisenaire Company of America, Inc. Copyright © 1978

★ Worksheet 49

Name _____

"Stand rods on end to build a plus table."

+	W	R	G	P	Y	D	K	N	E
W									
R									
G									
P									
Y									
D									
K									
N									
E									

"Use numerals to make an addition table."

+	1	2	3	4	5	6	7	8	9
1									
2									
3									
4									
5									
6									
7									
8									
9									

Building an Addition Table

Commentary in Teacher Resource Guide, p.117
One-Digit Addition and Subtraction with Cuisenaire Rods
Cuisenaire Company of America, Inc. Copyright © 1978

Worksheet **50**

This blank page indicates a break in the sequence of worksheets. Refer to the Teacher Resource Guide for the Learning Experiences which follow.

Name _____

"Find the sums."

   ①   3+5= _____

   ②   6+3= _____

   ③   1+7= _____

   ④   4+3= _____

   ⑤   2+2= _____

   ⑥   2+3= _____

   ⑦   5+5= _____

   ⑧   4+0= _____

"Check your answers with rods."

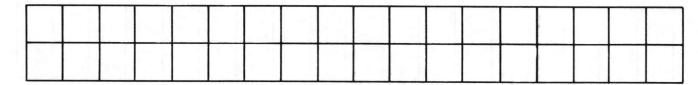

Name _____

'Find the sums."

    ①   1+2= _____

    ②   3+7= _____

    ③   4+4= _____

    ④   5+4= _____

    ⑤   2+8= _____

    ⑥   3+3= _____

    ⑦   6+1= _____

    ⑧   0+9= _____

'Check your answers with rods."

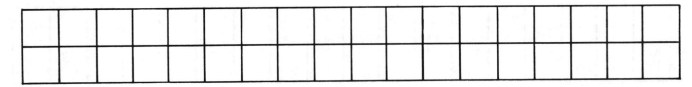

Checking Sums Through Ten
Commentary in Teacher Resource Guide, p.119
One-Digit Addition and Subtraction with Cuisenaire Rods
Cuisenaire Company of America, Inc. Copyright © 1978

Worksheet 52

Name _____

"Find the missing rod.
   Color the completed picture."

Example: _____

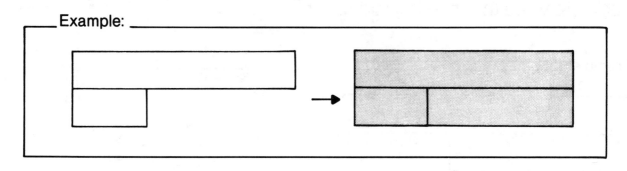

①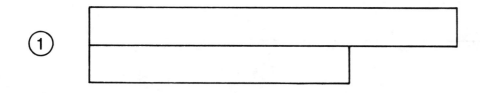

②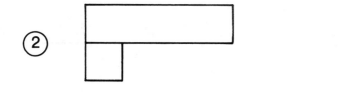

③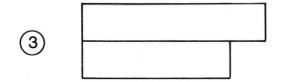

④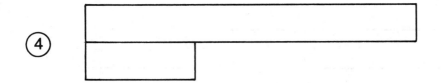

Commentary in Teacher Resource Guide, p.127
One-Digit Addition and Subtraction with Cuisenaire Rods
Cuisenaire Company of America, Inc. Copyright © 1978

Name _____

"Find the rods to match each rod picture.
Color each rod picture.
Use codes to write the missing rod story."

Example:

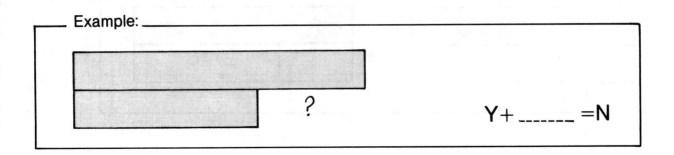

$Y + \text{_____} = N$

①

②

③

④

⑤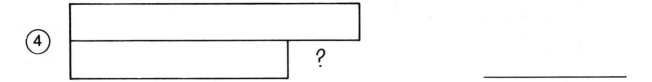

Practicing Missing Addends
Commentary in Teacher Resource Guide, p.127
One-Digit Addition and Subtraction with Cuisenaire Rods
Cuisenaire Company of America, Inc. Copyright © 1978

Name _____

"Color the rod picture for the missing rod story.
Use numerals to write the missing rod story.
Write the completed number story."

Example:

G+_____=Y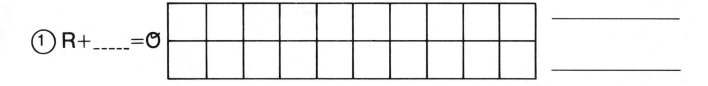

$$3+ \underline{} =5$$
$$3+ 2 =5$$

① R+_____=O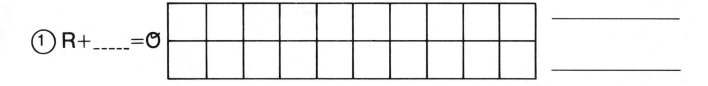
_____
_____

② K+_____=E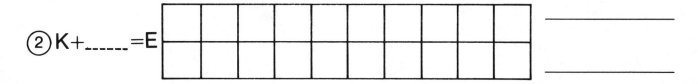
_____
_____

③ P+_____=N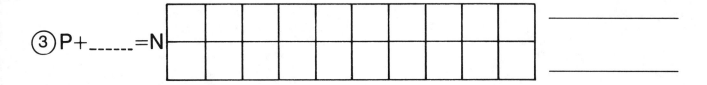
_____
_____

④ W+_____=D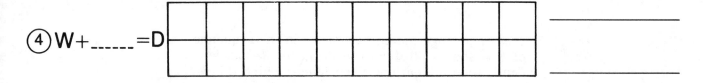
_____
_____

⑤ P+_____=K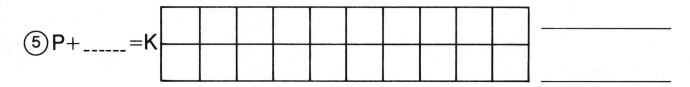
_____
_____

Commentary in Teacher Resource Guide, p.127
One-Digit Addition and Subtraction with Cuisenaire Rods
Cuisenaire Company of America, Inc. Copyright © 1978

This blank page indicates a break in the sequence of worksheets. Refer to the Teacher Resource Guide for the Learning Experiences which follow.

Name _____

"Color the correct rods to match the numerals.
Find and color the missing rod.
Write the completed story."

Example: _____

4+_____=7 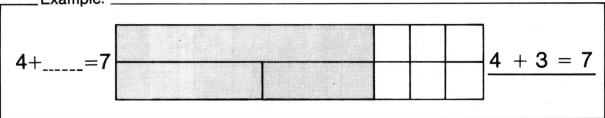 4 + 3 = 7

① 5+_____=10 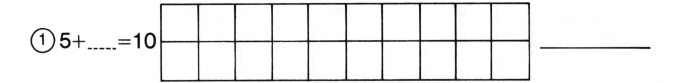 _____

② 2+_____=6 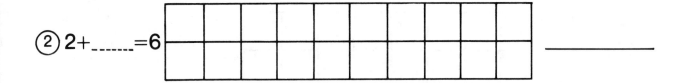 _____

③ 1+_____=10 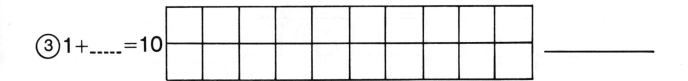 _____

④ 3+_____=8 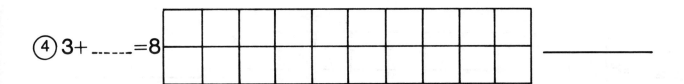 _____

⑤ 6+_____=9 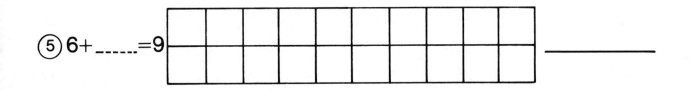 _____

Commentary in Teacher Resource Guide, p.129
One-Digit Addition and Subtraction with Cuisenaire Rods
Cuisenaire Company of America, Inc. Copyright © 1978

Name _____

"Color the correct rods to match the numerals.
 Find and color the missing rod.
 Write the completed story."

① 2+_____=8 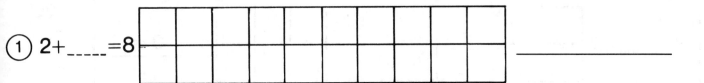 _____

② 5+_____=7 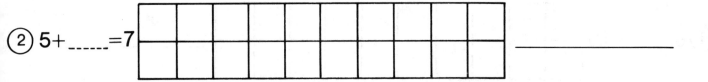 _____

③ 1+___=10 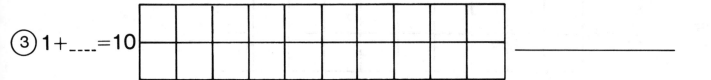 _____

④ 7+_____=9 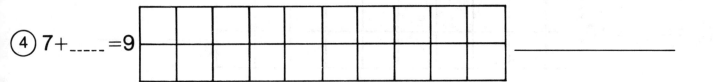 _____

⑤ 3+_____=6 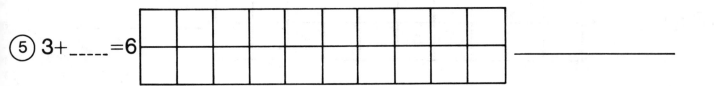 _____

Commentary in Teacher Resource Guide, p.129
One-Digit Addition and Subtraction with Cuisenaire Rods
Cuisenaire Company of America, Inc. Copyright © 1978

Name _____

"Complete the missing number stories."

    ①   3+ _____ =9

    ②   7+ _____ =8

    ③   1+ _____ =6

    ④   2+ _____ =4

    ⑤   9+ _____ =10

    ⑥   5+ _____ =10

    ⑦   4+ _____ =4

    ⑧   6+ _____ =7

"Check your answers with rods."

This blank page indicates a break in the sequence of worksheets. Refer to the Teacher Resource Guide for the Learning Experiences which follow.

"Listen to the teacher.
  Color the rods described.
  Complete the rod picture."

①

②

③

④

⑤

This blank page indicates a break in the sequence of worksheets. Refer to the Teacher Resource Guide for the Learning Experiences which follow.

Name _____

"Write the minus story for each rod picture."

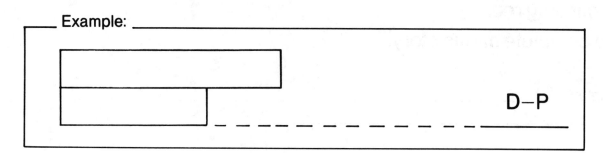

Example:

D−P

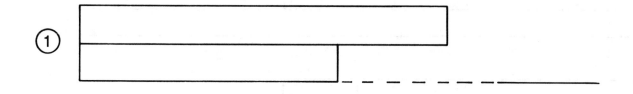

①

②

③

④

Name _____

"Write the minus story for each rod picture.

Find the missing rod.

Write the complete minus story."

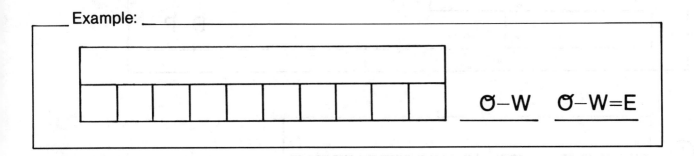

Example: _____

O—W _____ O—W=E _____

(1) 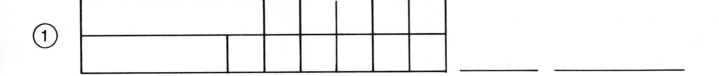 _____ _____

(2) _____ _____

(3) 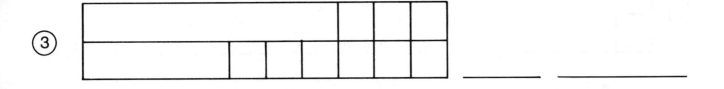 _____ _____

(4) 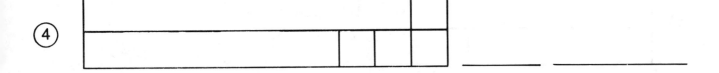 _____ _____

Commentary in Teacher Resource Guide, p.141
One-Digit Addition and Subtraction with Cuisenaire Rods
Cuisenaire Company of America, Inc. Copyright © 1978

Name _____

"Make some rod pictures showing minus stories.
  Write the minus story for each rod picture.
  Find the missing rod.
  Write the complete minus story."

(1) _____ _____ _____

(2) _____ _____ _____

(3) _____ _____ _____

(4) _____ _____ _____

(5) _____ _____ _____

This blank page indicates a break in the sequence
of worksheets. Refer to the Teacher Resource
Guide for the Learning Experiences which follow.

Name _____

"Color the minus story.

Write the subtraction story.

Write the completed subtraction story."

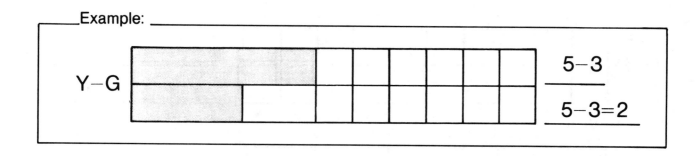

Example: _____

Y−G   5−3
        _____
        5−3=2

① O−Y 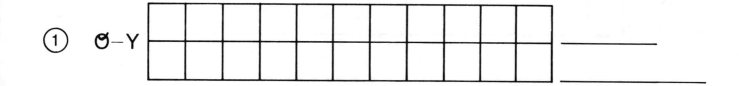 _____

② P−G 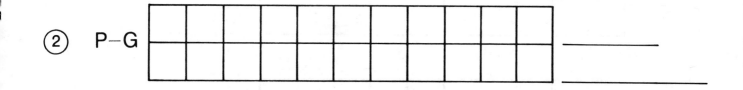 _____

③ G−W 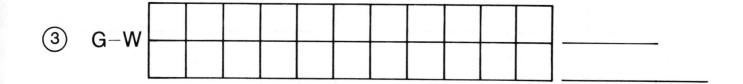 _____

④ N−N 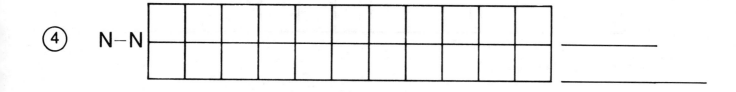 _____

Name _____

"Color the minus story.
  Write the subtraction story.
  Write the completed subtraction story."

① D–R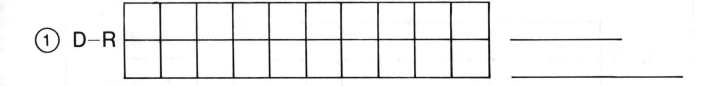

_____

_____

② K–P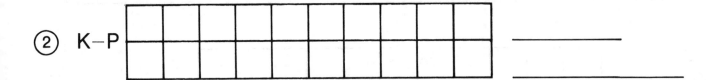

_____

_____

③ E–N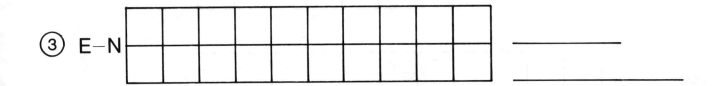

_____

_____

④ O–K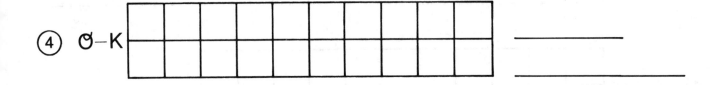

_____

_____

⑤ K–G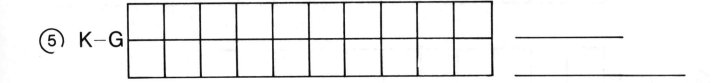

_____

_____

Writing Subtraction Stories   Worksheet **64**

Commentary in Teacher Resource Guide, p.143
One-Digit Addition and Subtraction with Cuisenaire Rods
Cuisenaire Company of America, Inc. Copyright © 1978

Name _____ ★ Worksheet **65**

"Write a minus story for rods.
Color your minus story.
Write the subtraction story.
Write the completed subtraction story."

① ___ — ___ 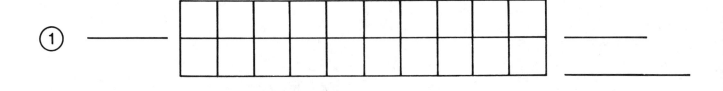 ___
___

② ___ — ___ 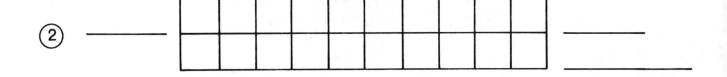 ___
___

③ ___ — ___ 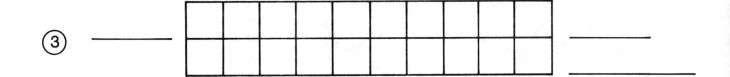 ___
___

④ ___ — ___  ___
___

⑤ ___ — ___ 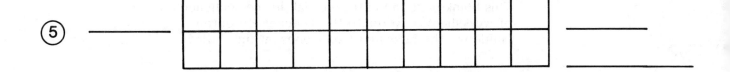 ___
___

Commentary in Teacher Resource Guide, p.143
One-Digit Addition and Subtraction with Cuisenaire Rods
Cuisenaire Company of America, Inc. Copyright © 1978

This blank page indicates a break in the sequence
of worksheets. Refer to the Teacher Resource
Guide for the Learning Experiences which follow.

Name _____

"Use rods on number lines to help find differences.

Write the completed subtraction stories."

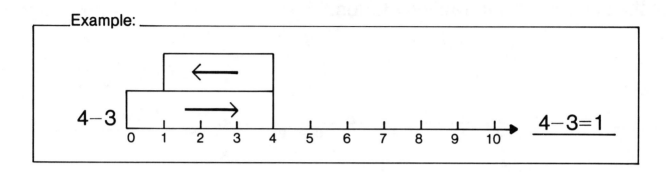

Example:

$4-3$ $4-3=1$

① $5-2$ 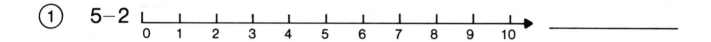 _____

② $10-3$ _____

③ $7-1$ _____

④ $6-3$ _____

⑤ $9-2$ _____

Commentary in Teacher Resource Guide, p.145
One-Digit Addition and Subtraction with Cuisenaire Rods
Cuisenaire Company of America, Inc. Copyright © 1978

Name _____

"Write some number stories for differences.
 Use rods on number lines to help find the differences.
 Write the completed subtraction stories."

① _____ 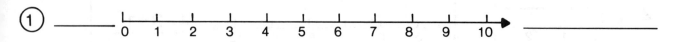 _____

② _____ 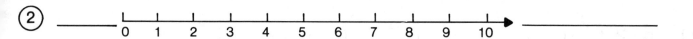 _____

③ _____ 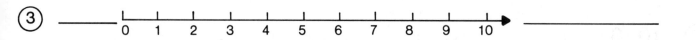 _____

④ _____ 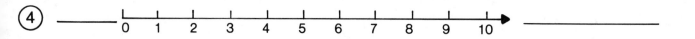 _____

⑤ _____ 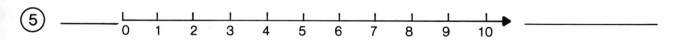 _____

⑥ _____ 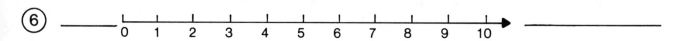 _____

Name _____

"Color the rod picture to match the number story.
Color the missing rod length.
Write the completed subtraction story."

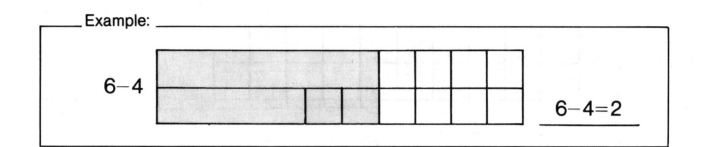

Example:

6−4

6−4=2

① 5−1 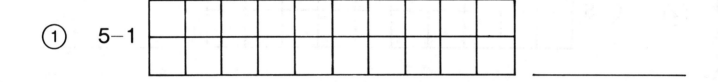 _____

② 4−2 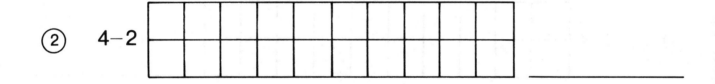 _____

③ 7−4 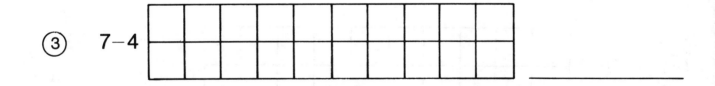 _____

④ 10−3 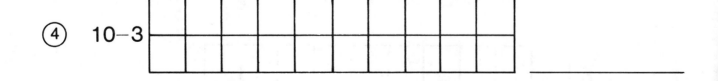 _____

Commentary in Teacher Resource Guide, p. 147
One-Digit Addition and Subtraction with Cuisenaire Rods
Cuisenaire Company of America, Inc. Copyright © 1978

Name _____

"Color the rod picture to match the number story.

Color the missing rod length.

Write the completed subtraction story."

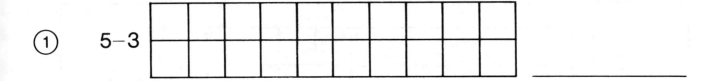

①   5−3   _____

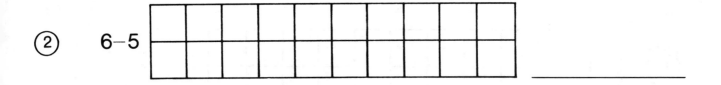

②   6−5   _____

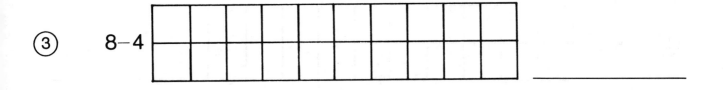

③   8−4   _____

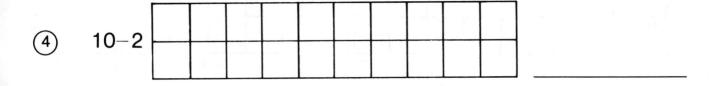

④   10−2   _____

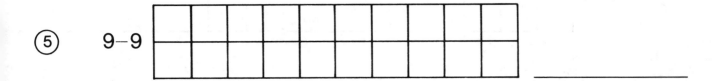

⑤   9−9   _____

Practicing Subtraction Stories   Worksheet **69**

Commentary in Teacher Resource Guide, p.147
One-Digit Addition and Subtraction with Cuisenaire Rods
Cuisenaire Company of America, Inc. Copyright © 1978

Name _____

"Write a number story for subtraction using numbers less than 10.

Color the rod picture to match the number story.

Color the missing rod length.

Write the completed subtraction story."

① _____   [grid]   _____

② _____   [grid]   _____

③ _____   [grid]   _____

④ _____   [grid]   _____

⑤ _____   [grid]   _____

Commentary in Teacher Resource Guide, p.147
One-Digit Addition and Subtraction with Cuisenaire Rods
Cuisenaire Company of America, Inc. Copyright © 1978

This blank page indicates a break in the sequence
of worksheets. Refer to the Teacher Resource
Guide for the Learning Experiences which follow.

Name _____

"Write an addition or subtraction story for each rod picture.
Rearrange the same three rods to make another rod story.
Write more addition and subtraction stories."

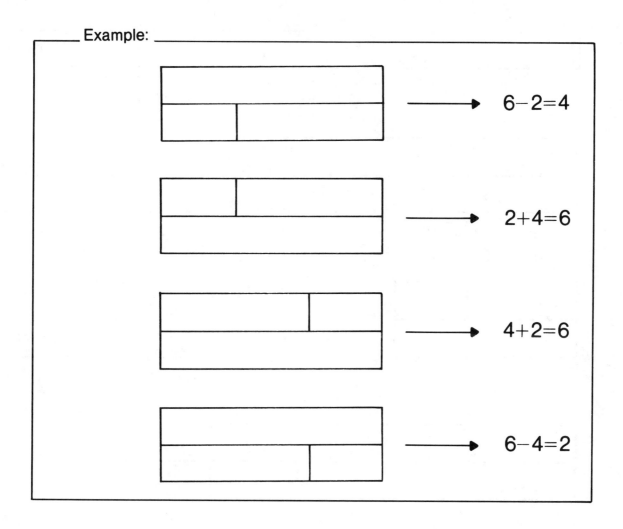

Example: _____

$6-2=4$

$2+4=6$

$4+2=6$

$6-4=2$

①

②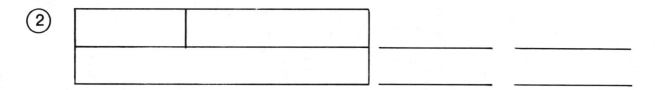

Commentary in Teacher Resource Guide, p.149
One-Digit Addition and Subtraction with Cuisenaire Rods
Cuisenaire Company of America, Inc. Copyright © 1978

Name _____

"Write addition and subtraction stories for each rod
picture and its various rearrangements."

① [rod picture]
 _____ _____
 _____ _____

② [rod picture]
 _____ _____
 _____ _____

③ [rod picture]
 _____ _____
 _____ _____

④ [rod picture]
 _____ _____
 _____ _____

⑤ [rod picture]
 _____ _____
 _____ _____

Commentary in Teacher Resource Guide, p.149
One-Digit Addition and Subtraction with Cuisenaire Rods
Cuisenaire Company of America, Inc. Copyright © 1978

Name _____

"Write all the addition and subtraction stories that can
be shown using the same three rods.

Use rods to help."

Example: _____

$1+7=8$

$7+1=8$

$8-1=7$

$8-7=1$

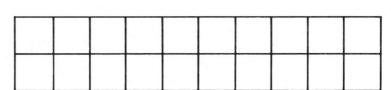

① $3+6=9$

_____

_____

_____

② $8+2=10$

_____

_____

_____

Commentary in Teacher Resource Guide, p.149
One-Digit Addition and Subtraction with Cuisenaire Rods
Cuisenaire Company of America, Inc. Copyright © 1978

This blank page indicates a break in the sequence
of worksheets. Refer to the Teacher Resource
Guide for the Learning Experiences which follow.

Name _____

"Match the white rods with an orange rod plus another rod.
  Write the plus story.
  Write the addition story."

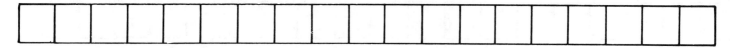

┌─ Example: ───┐
│   │
│   16   White Rods _ _ _ _ Ơ+ ___D___ _ _ _ _ 10+ ___6___ │
│   │
└───┘

① 19   White Rods _ _ _ _ Ơ+ _____ _ _ _ _ 10+ _____

② 11   White Rods _ _ _ _ Ơ+ _____ _ _ _ _ 10+ _____

③ 15   White Rods _ _ _ _ Ơ+ _____ _ _ _ _ 10+ _____

④ 12   White Rods _ _ _ _ Ơ+ _____ _ _ _ _ 10+ _____

⑤ 17   White Rods _ _ _ _ Ơ+ _____ _ _ _ _ 10+ _____

Name _____

"Match the white rods with an orange rod plus another rod.
Write the plus story.
Write an addition story."

①　18　White Rods ＿＿ ⦶+＿＿　＿＿＿ 10+＿＿＿＿＿

②　20　White Rods ＿＿ ⦶+＿＿　＿＿＿ 10+＿＿＿＿＿

③　15　White Rods ＿＿ ⦶+＿＿　＿＿＿ 10+＿＿＿＿＿

④　12　White Rods ＿＿ ⦶+＿＿　＿＿＿ 10+＿＿＿＿＿

⑤　14　White Rods ＿＿ ⦶+＿＿　＿＿＿ 10+＿＿＿＿＿

⑥　13　White Rods ＿＿ ⦶+＿＿　＿＿＿ 10+＿＿＿＿＿

Commentary in Teacher Resource Guide, p.155
One-Digit Addition and Subtraction with Cuisenaire Rods
Cuisenaire Company of America, Inc. Copyright © 1978

Name _____

"Match each train picture with an orange rod plus
   another rod.
Record your answers with codes."

Example:

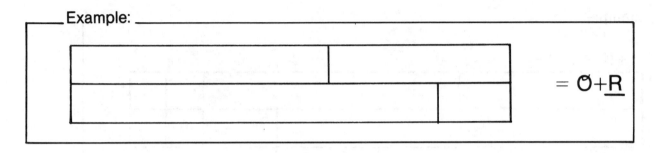

= O + <u>R</u>

① 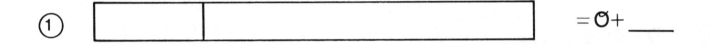 = O + ___

② = O + ___

③ = O + ___

④ = O + ___

⑤ = O + ___

⑥ = O + ___

Commentary in Teacher Resource Guide, p.159
One-Digit Addition and Subtraction with Cuisenaire Rods
Cuisenaire Company of America, Inc. Copyright © 1978

Name _____

"Color each train.

Match each train with an orange rod plus another rod.

Record the results with codes."

___ Example: ___

Y+K = O̶+R

① D+N = _____

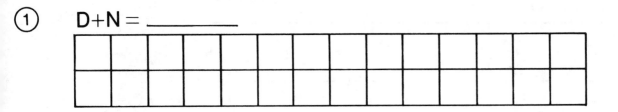

② K+K = _____

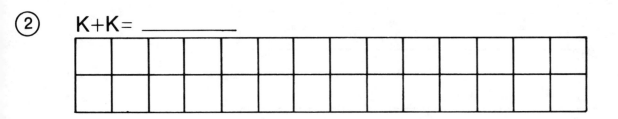

③ E+G = _____

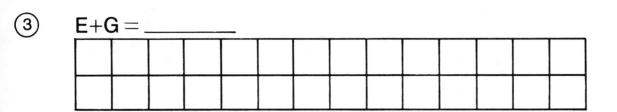

Commentary in Teacher Resource Guide, p.159
One-Digit Addition and Subtraction with Cuisenaire Rods
Cuisenaire Company of America, Inc. Copyright © 1978

Name _____

"Color each train.

Find the orange plus train that will match.

Write the addition story."

┌─── Example: ──┐
│   │
│   N+K   8+7= 10+5=15   │
│   │
│   │
└──┘

① R+E   _____ = _____ = _____

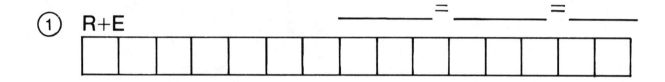

② N+D   _____ = _____ = _____

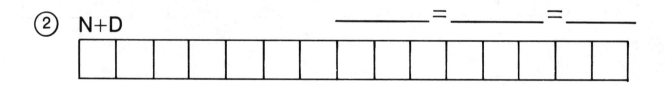

③ K+K   _____ = _____ = _____

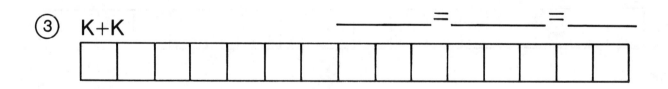

④ Y+D   _____ = _____ = _____

Commentary in Teacher Resource Guide, p.161
One-Digit Addition and Subtraction with Cuisenaire Rods
Cuisenaire Company of America, Inc. Copyright © 1978

Name _____

"Color each train.

Find the orange plus train that will match.

Write the addition story."

1 G+N   _____ = _____ = _____
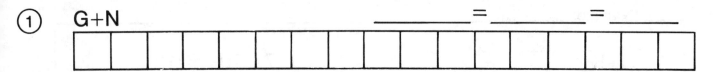

2 P+E   _____ = _____ = _____
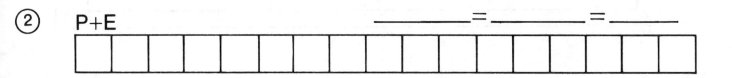

3 Y+K   _____ = _____ = _____
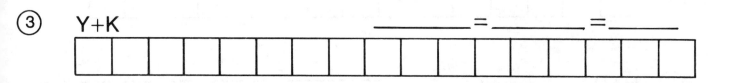

4 E+N   _____ = _____ = _____
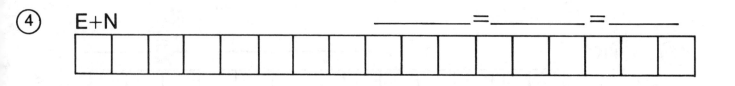

5 K+P+G   _____ = _____ = _____
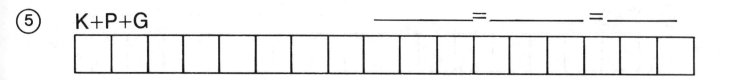

Writing Addition Stories
Commentary in Teacher Resource Guide, p. 161
One-Digit Addition and Subtraction with Cuisenaire Rods
Cuisenaire Company of America, Inc. Copyright © 1978

Worksheet **79**

Name _____

"Find each sum.

Use your rods to help."

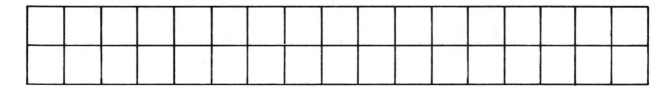

┌─── Example: ─────────────────────────────────────┐
│   │
│   8+3   │
│   8+3=11   │
│   │
└──┘

   ①   7+5 = _____

   ②   9+6 = _____

   ③   5+6 = _____

   ④   7+9 = _____

   ⑤   7
           + 8
           ‾‾‾‾

   ⑥   10
          + 2
          ‾‾‾‾

Commentary in Teacher Resource Guide, p.161
One-Digit Addition and Subtraction with Cuisenaire Rods
Cuisenaire Company of America, Inc. Copyright © 1978

This blank page indicates a break in the sequence
of worksheets. Refer to the Teacher Resource
Guide for the Learning Experiences which follow.

Name _____

"Make an addition table.
  Fill in all the sums."

+	1	2	3	4	5	6	7	8	9	10
1										
2										
3										
4										
5										
6										
7										
8										
9										
10										

"Use your rods to check the sums."

This blank page indicates a break in the sequence of worksheets. Refer to the Teacher Resource Guide for the Learning Experiences which follow.

Name _____

"Find each sum.
  Do not use rods."

           ①   6+7 = _____

           ②   5+9 = _____

           ③   8+8 = _____

           ④   3+10 = _____

           ⑤   7+7 = _____

           ⑥   9+8 = _____

           ⑦ $\begin{array}{r} 6 \\ +6 \\ \hline \end{array}$

"Check your answers with rods or rod pictures."

Commentary in Teacher Resource Guide, p.165
One-Digit Addition and Subtraction with Cuisenaire Rods
Cuisenaire Company of America, Inc. Copyright © 1978

This blank page indicates a break in the sequence
of worksheets. Refer to the Teacher Resource
Guide for the Learning Experiences which follow.

Name _____

"Find each sum.
Use rods or rod pictures to help."

① 4+1+5   4+1+5= _____

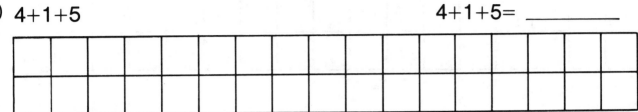

② 6+0+2   6+0+2= _____

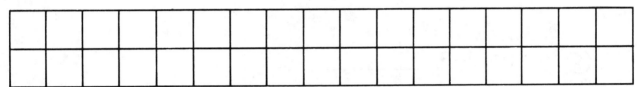

③ 4+4+6   4+4+6= _____

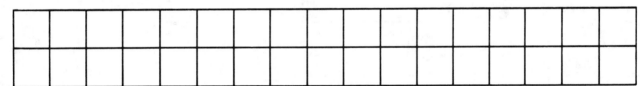

④ 7+3+5   7+3+5= _____

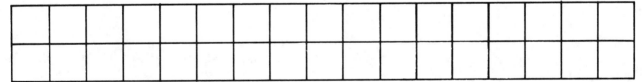

⑤ 8+9+1   8+9+1= _____

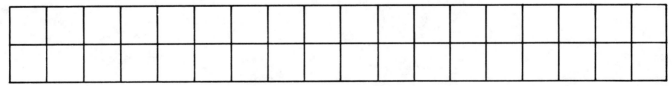

Finding Sums with More Than Two Addends   Worksheet **83**
Commentary in Teacher Resource Guide, p.167
One-Digit Addition and Subtraction with Cuisenaire Rods
Cuisenaire Company of America, Inc. Copyright © 1978

Name _____

"Find each sum.

Use rods or rod pictures to help."

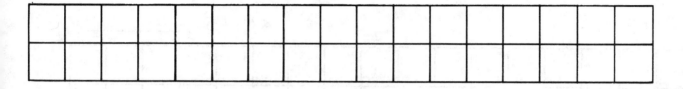

   ①   9+3+1= _____

   ②   10+2+3= _____

   ③   6+5+7= _____

               5

   ④   5

             + 7

               2

   ⑤   7

            +9

Finding Sums with More Than Two Addends

Commentary in Teacher Resource Guide, p.167
One-Digit Addition and Subtraction with Cuisenaire Rods
Cuisenaire Company of America, Inc. Copyright © 1978

Worksheet **84**

Name _____

"Find each sum."

①   2+3+4= _____

②   6+1+2= _____

③   2+7+5= _____

④   5+5+3= _____

⑤   7+8+5= _____

⑥   6+5+4= _____

⑦   3+8+0= _____

⑧   8+2+10= _____

"Use rods to check your answers."

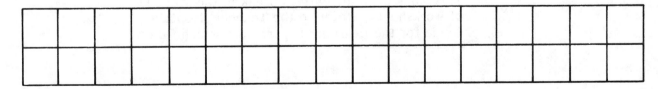

Finding Sums with More Than Two Addends

Commentary in Teacher Resource Guide, p.167
One-Digit Addition and Subtraction with Cuisenaire Rods
Cuisenaire Company of America, Inc. Copyright © 1978

Worksheet **85**

This blank page indicates a break in the sequence
of worksheets. Refer to the Teacher Resource
Guide for the Learning Experiences which follow.

Name _____

"Cover the design with rods.

Find the number value for each design.

Write an addition story for the design.

Cover the design in a different way to check your answer."

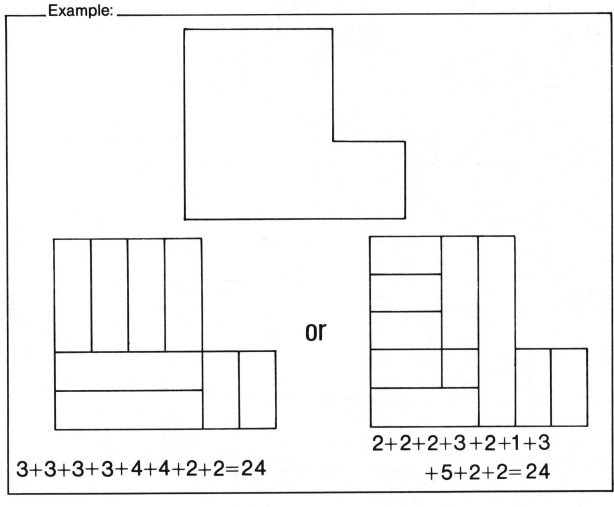

Example:

or

3+3+3+3+4+4+2+2=24

2+2+2+3+2+1+3
+5+2+2=24

"Cover each design with rods.

Find the number value for each design.

Write an addition story for each design."

①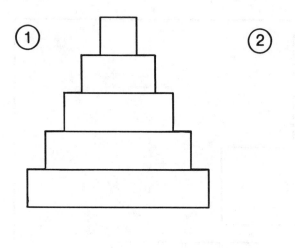

②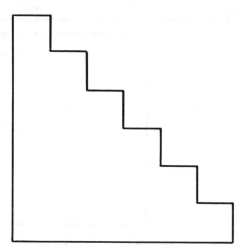

③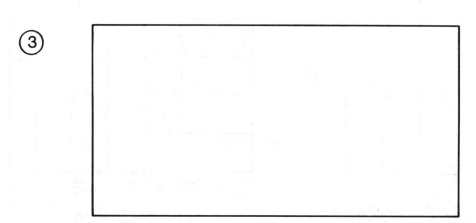

④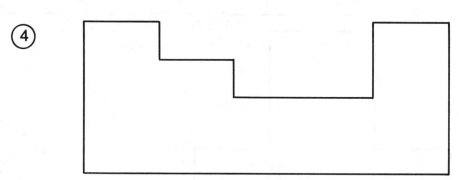

Commentary in Teacher Resource Guide, p.169
One-Digit Addition and Subtraction with Cuisenaire Rods
Cuisenaire Company of America, Inc. Copyright © 1978

Name _____

"Color the rod picture for each subtraction story.

Find the difference.

Write the completed subtraction story."

Example: _____

12−5   12−5=7

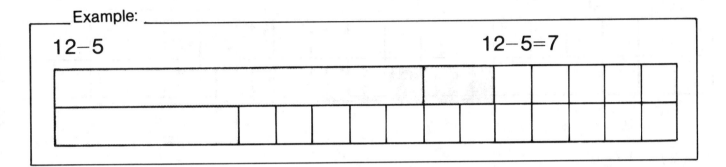

① 18−9   _____

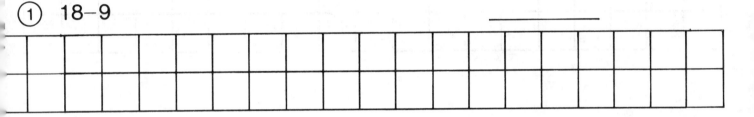

② 13−6   _____

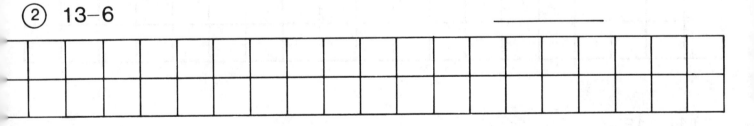

③ 20−7   _____

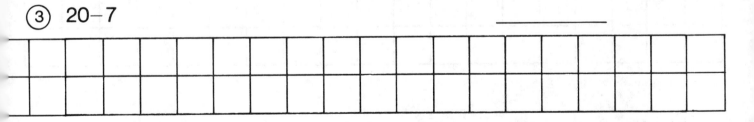

Commentary in Teacher Resource Guide, p.179
One-Digit Addition and Subtraction with Cuisenaire Rods
Cuisenaire Company of America, Inc. Copyright © 1978

Name _____

"Color the rod picture for each subtraction story.
Find the difference.
Write the completed subtraction story."

(1) 11−5   _____

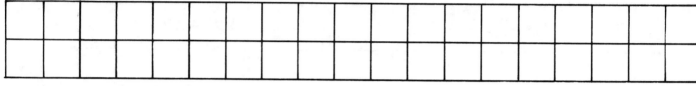

(2) 17−7   _____

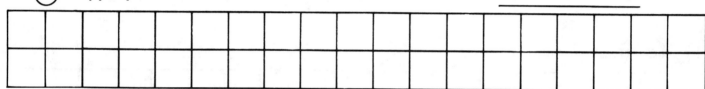

(3) 14−9   _____

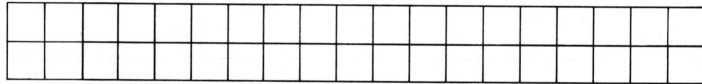

(4) 18−2   _____

(5) 15−6   _____

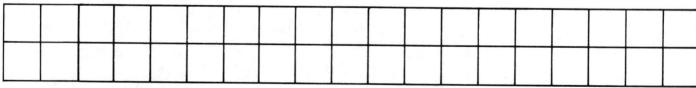

Commentary in Teacher Resource Guide, p.179
One-Digit Addition and Subtraction with Cuisenaire Rods
Cuisenaire Company of America, Inc. Copyright © 1978

Name _____

"Write a subtraction story starting with a number greater than 10.

Color the rod picture for each subtraction story.

Find the difference.

Write the completed subtraction story."

① _____   _____

② _____   _____

③ _____   _____

④ _____   _____

⑤ _____   _____

Name _____

Find each difference.

Use the rods to help."

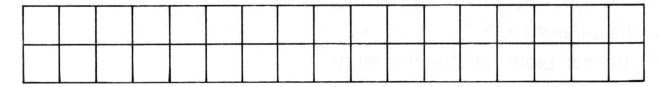

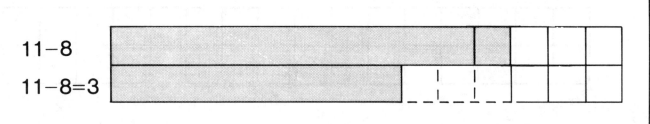

Example: _____

| 11−8 | |
| 11−8=3 | |

① 12−9= _____

② 16−7= _____

③ 11−2= _____

④ 13−8= _____

⑤ 15−4= _____

⑥   16
   − 8
   ‾‾‾‾

⑦   20
   − 8
   ‾‾‾‾

⑧   12
   −2
   ‾‾‾‾

Commentary in Teacher Resource Guide, p.179
One-Digit Addition and Subtraction with Cuisenaire Rods
Cuisenaire Company of America, Inc. Copyright © 1978

Name _____

"Find each difference.
Do not use rods."

    ① $16-3=$ _____

    ② $12-7=$ _____

    ③ $15-8=$ _____

    ④ $20-3=$ _____

⑤
$$\begin{array}{r} 11 \\ -9 \\ \hline \end{array}$$

⑦
$$\begin{array}{r} 20 \\ -8 \\ \hline \end{array}$$

⑥
$$\begin{array}{r} 13 \\ -7 \\ \hline \end{array}$$

⑧
$$\begin{array}{r} 17 \\ -8 \\ \hline \end{array}$$

"Check your answers with rods or rod pictures."

Checking Subtraction Stories   Worksheet 92

Commentary in Teacher Resource Guide, p.181
One-Digit Addition and Subtraction with Cuisenaire Rods
Cuisenaire Company of America, Inc. Copyright © 1978

This blank page indicates a break in the sequence
of worksheets. Refer to the Teacher Resource
Guide for the Learning Experiences which follow.

Name _____

"For each rod picture write the plus or minus story."

Example:
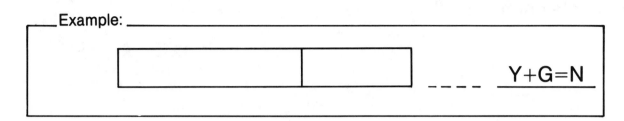
Y+G=N

①  - - - - - - - - _____

②  - - - - - - - - _____

③ 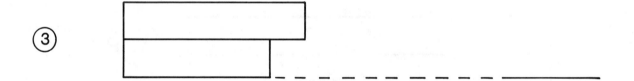 - - - - - - - - _____

④ 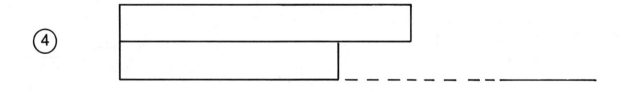 - - - - - - - - _____

⑤  - - - - - - - - _____

Commentary in Teacher Resource Guide, p.183
One-Digit Addition and Subtraction with Cuisenaire Rods
Cuisenaire Company of America, Inc. Copyright © 1978

Name _____

"Match each rod picture with the correct plus or minus story
Complete each story."

①   O−K= _____

② 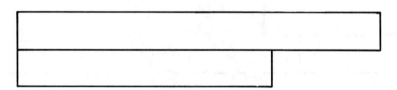   E+W= _____

③   R−W= _____

④   Y−R= _____

⑤ 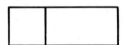   Y+R= _____

⑥ 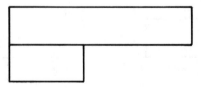   W+ R= _____

Commentary in Teacher Resource Guide, p.183
One-Digit Addition and Subtraction with Cuisenaire Rods
Cuisenaire Company of America, Inc. Copyright © 1978

Name _____

"For each number story, color the rod picture.
Write the completed number story."

Example:

$10-7$ $10-7=3$

① $4+5$ _____

② $2+6$ _____

③ $8-1$ _____

④ $3+2$ _____

⑤ $10-3$ _____

Mastering Addition and Subtraction   Worksheet 95
Commentary in Teacher Resource Guide, p.185
One-Digit Addition and Subtraction with Cuisenaire Rods
Cuisenaire Company of America, Inc. Copyright © 1978

Name _____

'For each number story, color the rod picture.
Write the completed number story.''

Example:

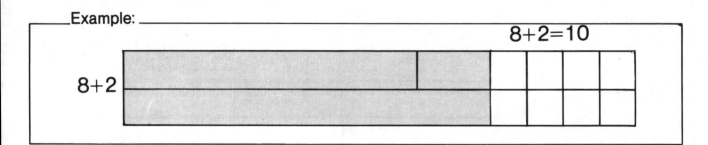

8+2=10

8+2

① 7+3

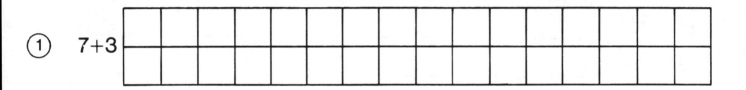

② 9+4

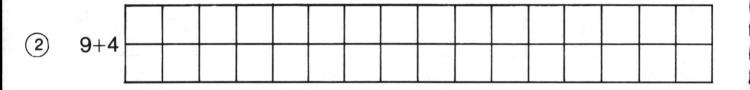

③ 11
   −2

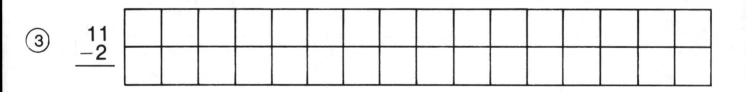

④ 1
   +2
   +3

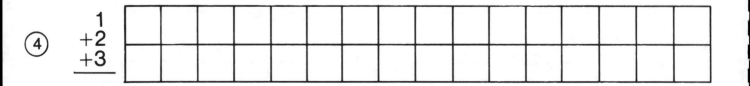

Mastering Addition and Subtraction
Commentary in Teacher Resource Guide, p.185
One-Digit Addition and Subtraction with Cuisenaire Rods
Cuisenaire Company of America, Inc. Copyright © 1978

Worksheet 96